Dd   Ee   Ff

Kk   Ll   Mm

Qq Rr Ss Tt

Xx   Yy   Zz

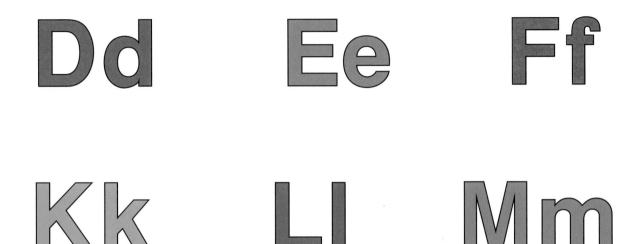

Presented to

from

Dear Parents:

This first alphabet book will delight young children ages two to six years. Baby Bop plays with familiar objects representing the letters of the alphabet. Preschool children begin recognizing letters and develop a growing interest in printed words. The simple rhyming text and brightly colored illustrations will encourage young children to "read" along and have fun.

We consider books to be life-long gifts that develop and enhance the love of reading. We hope you enjoy reading along with Barney and Baby Bop.

Mary Ann Dudko, Ph.D.
Margie Larsen, M.Ed.
Early Childhood Educational Specialists

Editor: Linda Hartley, M.Ed.
Art Director/Designer: Tricia Legault

©1993 by The Lyons Group

PUBLISHING
A Division of The Lyons Group
300 East Bethany Drive, Allen, Texas 75002

Barney™ and Baby Bop™ are trademarks of The Lyons Group.

1 2 3 4 5 6 7 8 9 10   97 96 95 94 93

ISBN 1-57064-008-4

Library of Congress Number 93-77869

Baby Bop's
ABC
BOOK

Written by Mark Bernthal   Illustrated by Larry Daste

Aa

A is for **a**pple,
so shiny and red.

Bb

B is for **b**utterfly,
near Baby Bop's head.

Cc

C is for cat,
sound asleep in the sun.

Dd

D is for **d**olls,
having tea party fun.

Ee

E is for **e**lephant -
big ears, trunk, and feet.

Ff

F is for **f**lowers
that smell, oh, so sweet.

Gg

G is for gorillas,
dancing with glee.

Hh

H is for **h**at,
as floppy as can be!

Ii

I is for **i**gloo,
a house made of ice.

J is for jacket,
so snuggly and nice.

Kk

K is for kite,
flying high in the sky.

Ll

L is for lamb,
running playfully by.

Mm

M is for **m**oon,
shining so bright.

Nn

N is for **n**est,
birdies say, "Night, night!"

O is for octopus,
drawing a mouse.

Pp

P is for **p**aint.
Baby Bop paints a house.

Qq

Q is for **q**uilt,
pretty pieces together.

Rr

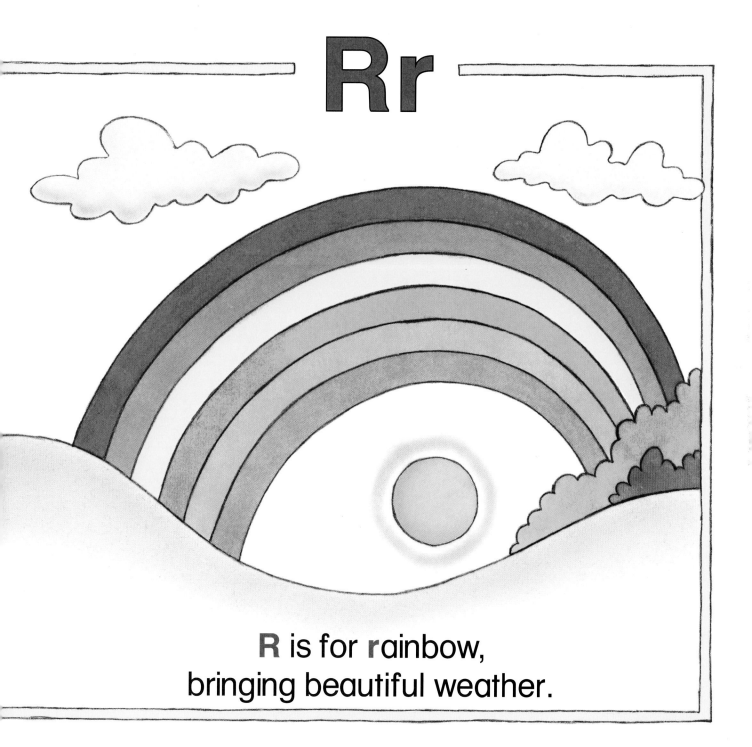

R is for **r**ainbow,
bringing beautiful weather.

S is for **s**un,
peeking out from a cloud.

Tt

T is for **t**ruck.
Vrooom - it's so loud!

Uu

U is for **u**mbrella,
keeping Baby Bop dry.

Vv

V is for **v**est.
Teddy's vest looks like his tie.

Ww

W is for **w**agon,
taking friends for a ride.

X is for e**x**it.
Let's all go outside!

Yy

Y is for yo-yo,
spinning up and down.

Z is for **z**ebra,
prancing off to town.

Aa Bb Cc

Gg Hh Ii Jj

Nn Oo Pp

Uu Vv Ww